TEXAS
REBEL

by Rita Kerr

EAKIN PRESS ★ AUSTIN, TEXAS

Published in the United States of America
By Eakin Press, P.O. Box 23069, Austin, Texas 78735

ISBN 0-89015-695-5

Library of Congress Cataloging-in-Publication Data
Kerr, Rita.
  Texas rebel / by Rita Kerr.
      p.   cm.
  Summary: A fictionalized biography of Churchill Roberts, a second-generation Texan who joined the Thirteenth Cavalry Battalion during the Civil War and fought in Texas, Arkansas, and Louisiana.
  ISBN (invalid) 0-89015-695-5 : $8.95
  1. Roberts, Churchill — Juvenile fiction. 2. United States — History — Civil War, 1861–1865 — Juvenile fiction. [1. Roberts, Churchill — Fiction. 2. United States — History — Civil War, 1861–1865 — Fiction. 3. Texas — History — 1846–1950 — Fiction.]
  I. Title.
PZ7.K468458Tc   1989
[Fic] — dc19   88-37539
                                                                         CIP
                                                                          AC

This book is dedicated to the author's great-grandfather,
Churchill Roberts,
and to those who fought
in the Civil War.

Acknowledgments

The author wishes to thank the following people for their words of encouragement and interest in *Texas Rebel*: Linda Reid, Beverly Roberts, Millie Foster, Kathy Dworaczyk, and Jamie and Joie Baker.

Contents

Preface

Churchill Roberts, a loyal citizen of Texas, had deep roots in the land. A second-generation Texan, his parents and grandparents had come with Stephen F. Austin's first colony in 1823 and settled along the Brazos River.

Shortly after the outbreak of the Civil War, Churchill and his brother James joined Major Waller's Thirteenth Cavalry Battalion of Texas. The group fought in Louisiana and Texas, as well as briefly in Arkansas. During those war years, Churchill had a number of adventures. When the fighting ended in 1865, Churchill returned home to his sweetheart, Elizabeth Susan Newman. *Texas Rebel* is based on true facts pertaining to the life of Churchill Roberts.

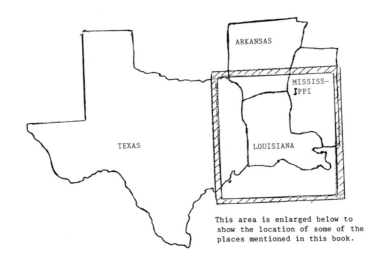

This area is enlarged below to show the location of some of the places mentioned in this book.

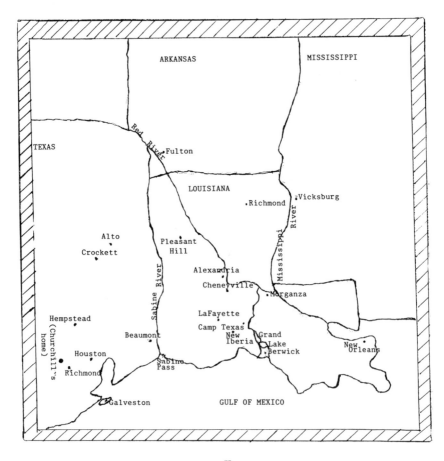

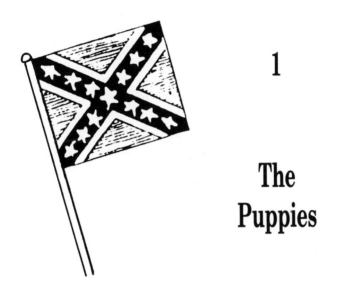

1

The Puppies

"Aw, Ma, why can't I have a puppy?"

"Because we do not need another dog. We have Job." Elizabeth Roberts pushed back the lock of hair from her forehead and stared at her oldest son. Churchill was so like his father, with his thick black hair and dark brown eyes. Little Liz and James, Elizabeth's other children, had her blue eyes and blond curls. She shook her finger as she added, "And don't you argue with me, Churchill Roberts!"

The boy stared in silence at his half-eaten breakfast. He did not feel hungry. His younger brother spoke up, "But, Ma, Job is getting old. That dog just sleeps and eats and wags his tail. He is no fun."

"James is right," Churchill said hopefully. "Remember how you cried when your old dog Rex died? That was when Pa decided to get Job. Now Job is getting old. He will die one of these days. We need a puppy to take his place . . ."

"Humph! With this new baby coming, the last thing in the world we need around here is another dog," his mother replied.

Churchill toyed with the cold biscuit on his plate. He was thinking of how much he wanted a puppy — one that he could train and call his own. He decided to try again. "Ma, don't you understand? This wouldn't be an ordinary dog. It would be one of the finest. David Randon said he would give me a puppy for helping him pick his cotton. This pup would be special. Everybody knows that Mr. Randon raises the best horses and hound dogs in Texas!"

His mother threw up her hands in dismay. "Now that is just what we need! A hound dog baying to the moon; howling all night and keeping us awake."

"But . . ." Churchill did not finish. His mother's face told him he had said enough — maybe too much. In despair he looked across the table to his father. His father winked. That was their secret signal that everything would be all right.

"Churchill, don't say another word. The matter is closed. I have work to do. You boys help your sister clear the table. William," she glanced toward her husband, "have you forgotten this is wash day?"

"No, dear," William said, pushing back his chair from the table. "I know it's Monday. I was just leaving. You boys help your mother." He hurried out the door heading for the wood pile to grab an armload of wood.

William stacked the wood in the usual place in the yard and started a fire. Once it was burning brightly, he picked up the buckets and headed for the well. As he filled the washtubs with water, he thought about his sons. He did not blame them for hating housework, but their little sister was too small to be of much help. Liz was only six. With the fourth child due any day, Elizabeth needed help. Her niece would come over to stay for a while when the baby arrived. In the meantime, the boys had to help.

Mondays and Tuesdays were not Churchill's favorite

days of the week. He hated wash day. It was not easy keeping the fire burning under the pot of boiling water. It was hard work bending over the steaming washpot to poke the clothes with a long pole to loosen the dirt. Once they were clean, the clothes had to be lifted out with the pole into the tubs of cool water. After their mother determined that the clothes were rinsed clean, the boys squeezed the water out of the clothes and spread them around on the bushes to dry.

The boys were usually soaking wet by the time they had finished. Even on the sunniest days, the high humidity kept the heavy cotton garments from getting completely dry. This meant they had to be spread around the cabin before nightfall in hopes they would be dry enough to iron.

The next day the boys took turns carrying loads of wood to keep the fire going in the fireplace in order to heat the heavy metal irons. Ironing was not easy, either. Elizabeth ironed until she became tired, then one of the boys took over the job. Churchill secretly hoped the new baby would be a girl so she could grow up and help around the house.

A few mornings after their discussion about the puppy, Elizabeth said, "Son, are you sure Mr. Randon said he would give you a puppy?"

Churchill nodded.

"Well, do you promise to take care of him? You won't let him chase the chickens or ruin my flowers or dig in the garden?"

"Oh, Ma," Churchill cried excitedly, "I promise. If you will let me have one, I'll see that he is the best dog in the world!"

"All right," his mother sighed. "Your father feels you should have a puppy. But remember — that dog stays outside. I do not want it in the house."

Churchill's eyes filled with gratitude. His father smiled. "Children, we have told you stories about Tex and Rex. Those two dogs were an important part of our

3

lives when your mother and I were young. When they died it was like losing part of the family." William's eyes grew misty and he added, "I think every boy should have a pup to call his own." He looked from Churchill to his younger son. "Boys, I am going to the field now but I'll be back early. I reckon the oxen could use a rest. When I return we will saddle up the horses and ride over to the Randons. I haven't seen our neighbors for some time."

The Roberts and Randon families had been friends for years. Twenty-five years earlier, in 1823, William and Elizabeth's families had come to Texas with David Randon and his brother John. They were among Stephen Austin's first colony. William's father, Noel Roberts, and Elizabeth's father, William Pryor, had been dead for a number of years. John Randon was gone too. William still valued David Randon's friendship, not because he was one of the richest men in Texas, but because he was a good neighbor.

Before he left for the field, William looked at Churchill. "Son, maybe you had better fix a bed for the puppy out here on the porch. It will be late when we get home tonight. See if you can find a piece of rope too. Remember, it is natural for a hound to follow its nose. You don't want that pup chasing off after the scent of some animal before you get him trained."

Churchill wondered if the morning would never end. He kept thinking about a name for his puppy as he put one of his mother's old quilts in the bed he had fixed. Once his father returned, Churchill helped saddle their horses. After a hurried meal, the boys and their father waved goodbye and rode off toward the south.

When they reached Mill Creek, they paused to let the horses get a drink of water. Churchill and James knew every inch of the creek. That was where they fished and went swimming. Sometimes they hunted squirrels by the creek. Churchill tingled with excitement as he thought of the days ahead. He could go hunting with his dog. With a hound's keen sense of smell, no telling what they might find.

They came to the pile of rocks that marked the beginning of their neighbor's land. They were still some distance from his house. The Randons, like most of the early settlers, received a land grant when they came to Texas. David Randon owned over a league of land, more than 4,428 acres. The Randons and most of their neighbors raised cotton and corn. Many had slaves to work the land. Churchill was happy his folks could not afford to own slaves. He felt that slavery was wrong.

The workers in the cotton fields waved at them as the three rode by. The riders waved back. As they neared the Randons' house, they heard dogs barking from their kennels behind the house. Churchill saw a number of smaller cabins in the distance. The workers lived there.

The early Texas houses consisted of two log cabins or rooms side by side with a porch joining them. They called the porch or breezeway the dog run. Churchill's home was built like that. The Randons, however, had built a new two-storied house. Churchill always wished his mother could have such a place until he thought of all the housework it would involve.

Mr. Randon and his wife Nancy came out of the house when they heard the dogs barking. After a brief exchange of greetings they sat on the porch to talk. The boys enjoyed the cool, sweet drinks and sugar cookies they were served. However, Churchill wondered if the men would never stop talking. He was eager to see the dogs. The men finally stood up to go to the kennels and the boys ran on ahead.

Churchill saw six tiny puppies huddled with their mother in the first cage. They were digging their little paws into their mother's stomach as they nursed. The babies were so young that their eyes were not yet opened. Churchill wondered how their short legs would ever hold up their fat little furry bodies.

In the next cage there were five noisy, playful puppies. Churchill figured they were about six weeks old. They were too young to be taken from their mother since they were still nursing.

At the last cage, Mr. Randon paused. "Now these hounds are older. Since they have been weaned we put several litters together. Son," he looked at Churchill seriously, "before you decide, remember that the males grow to be larger and stronger but the females are usually more gentle and easier to train. Would you like to go inside the cage?"

The boys found themselves surrounded by more than a dozen lively, roly-poly puppies. They were coal black except for the tan markings above their eyes, on their heads, and down their sides. They all looked alike at first. But one caught Churchill's eye. It had the biggest feet, the longest ears, and the saddest eyes Churchill had ever seen. When he picked it up the puppy licked his face with its warm, pink tongue. The puppy's long tail swished from side to side, thumping against Churchill's chest.

"Well, son," his father said, "what do you think? Is that the one?" William already knew the answer.

"Oh, Pa. This is my dog. May I have this one? Please? I would call him Thumper. Just look at his tail!"

David Randon noticed the younger boy. He was cuddling a very small puppy in his arms and had a wistful look on his face. "So . . . you have taken a liking to Tiny, have you? We always call the runt of any litter Tiny. If this Tiny lives he will probably be too small to be of any use to me. What do you think, William? Can the boy have this runt?"

And so it was that each of the boys got a puppy of his own.

William realized it was getting late. He said it was time for them to go. By the time they reached home it was almost dark. The puppies were sleeping contentedly in the crooks of the boys' arms. They scarcely opened their eyes when the boys placed them side by side in their new bed on the porch. After eating a cold supper, the boys fell asleep listening to Thumper's snore just outside the door of their room.

6

*The boys found themselves surrounded by more than a dozen
lively, roly-poly puppies.*

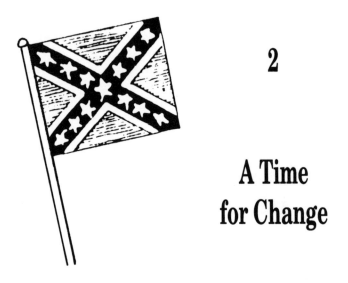

2

A Time
for Change

Life was hectic in the Roberts house after the new baby arrived. Liz was disappointed that she did not get the sister she had wanted. She decided little Billy would have to do. Churchill thought it strange anything so small could cause so much trouble. He was relieved when his cousin Mary came to help his mother.

Each evening after supper, William helped the boys with the puppies. They taught Thumper to roll over to play dead and to fetch a stick. No matter how hard he tried, poor little Tiny could not keep up with Thumper. James was furious when his sister called Tiny a runt. James loved his dog just the way it was. And although his mother and Liz would never have admitted it, they were fond of Tiny too. James was proud when his father called Tiny a spunky little critter.

One morning they discovered old Job had died in his sleep during the night. Although the children would miss the dog, William reminded them that Job had lived a full life. He was glad they had the puppies to take Job's place.

The warm days of spring turned to summer. In the afternoons, after their chores were done, Churchill and James headed for Mill Creek with their dogs. Thumper might have left them far behind had Churchill not had him on a rope. When they neared the creek, the puppies always whined and whimpered with their tails pointed in the air. That was a signal they had caught some scent. One afternoon they chanced upon a wild turkey near the creek bank. The hounds went wild. The frightened bird vanished quickly into the weeds before the boys could move.

As the summer drew to an end, the cotton fields turned white. There was little time for play after that. Picking cotton was hard, hot work, but the boys did not complain. Much of the cotton was loaded into the wagon to be taken down to the Brazos River, where it was put onto one of the barges that came by. The barges carried the cotton downriver some one hundred miles to the Gulf of Mexico. There the cotton was put onto a ship and taken to New Orleans to be sold. William and the other farmers needed money for supplies and the things they could not grow.

Fall and winter came and went. On Churchill's fourteenth birthday his father surprised him with a horse he could call his own. No one dreamed William was foretelling the future that day when he said, "Son, you are almost grown. You will soon be wearing my shoes."

Once the spring planting was finished, William and the boys began chopping down trees to build a larger barn. Their neighbors, the Fulshears, came over to help. William Roberts and Churchill Fulshear had been best friends since they were boys. In fact, William and Elizabeth had named their first son after him.

With William's two sons and Mr. Fulshear's two boys, the work on the barn moved quickly. One afternoon William was placing the final shingles on the roof. He

9

was kneeling with his back to the edge of the roof, putting a shingle into place. Suddenly, he felt himself slipping as he lost his balance. He clawed at the shingles with his fingers as he yelled for help.

The others came running. They froze in horror as they watched William's vain efforts to grab hold of the shingles to stop his slide. Once he reached the edge of the roof, William's body seemed to fly into the air. He hit the ground with a thud. His head hit the corner of one of the logs.

Churchill Fulshear was the first to reach William. He bent down to help, then discovered there was nothing he could do. The sharp edge of the log had pierced his friend's skull. William was dead.

The weeks that followed were like a bad dream. Neighbors and friends for miles around came to pay their respects. Churchill acted bravely, but he thought his heart would break. He missed his father more than anyone could ever know. His mother was overcome with grief too. Since he was the oldest child in the family, Churchill knew he must now step into his father's shoes. He had to be the man of the house. Churchill tried to assume the role. It was not easy.

During sickness and sorrow, work always waited to be done. The boys worked long hours in the field, trying to keep the weeds from ruining the cotton. Elizabeth watched them leave early in the morning and return bone-tired in the evening. She knew it was too much for them, but there was nothing that she could do.

Early one morning David Randon surprised them with a visit. The boys were proud when he bragged on what a fine job they were doing raising the dogs.

Before he left, Mr. Randon put his arm around Elizabeth and looked down into her face. With fatherly kindness he said, "Betsy, I know the boys are doing their best, but you all need a man around here. I have a fellow working for me that might be the answer to your problem. His name is Marcus Harry. I don't need Marcus right now.

You see, my sister's son, Thomas Newman, came from Alabama and he has been helping me. Would you like for me to send Marcus over? He seems like a bright young man. As I recall, his folks came to Texas back in 1838. They are dead now. The fellow has no family. He is alone."

Elizabeth quickly agreed that she would like to talk to Marcus Harry.

As he was leaving, Mr. Randon smiled. "By the way, I forgot to tell you the latest gossip. It seems my nephew Thomas has taken a liking to your niece Mary. I guess it was love at first sight. I wouldn't be surprised if those two got married before long."

Elizabeth was pleased. She liked her niece. Mary was much like her mother, Elizabeth's older sister Harriet.

At noon the next day the family was gathered around the table when the dogs began barking. It was Marcus Harry. Elizabeth insisted he come in and have something to eat. After they were finished, Churchill rode with him around the fields. Marcus could see there was too much work for Churchill and his brother. He agreed to stay and lend them a hand. Since there was no place but the boys' room for him to sleep, he moved in with them.

The family found it difficult having a stranger around the house at first. But, fortunately, Marcus was a likable fellow. He bragged on Elizabeth's cooking, told lively stories to make the children laugh, and played with the dogs when the chores were done. Marcus found a place in their hearts before the month was over.

One morning Churchill chanced to look at his mother. Her eyes were no longer swollen. He knew she had been crying herself to sleep since his father's death. Now she was actually smiling! With the shortage of women in Texas, Churchill felt certain his mother was too young and too beautiful to stay a widow for long. With four children to raise, she needed a husband.

Marcus and the boys worked hard. That fall when they brought in the harvest, Elizabeth was delighted. They had a bumper crop of cotton and corn. Elizabeth announced that they would celebrate by going to Richmond to buy supplies. The children were excited. Going to town was a rare treat.

Early the next morning, after breakfast, they hitched the horses to the wagon. Churchill sat in the back with the younger children. His mother rode on the seat with Marcus. Elizabeth was wearing her best dress and had combed her hair so that curls framed her face. A sprig of wild daisies was pinned to the brim of her bonnet. She looked too young to be Churchill's mother.

As the wagon squeaked over the bumpy, dusty road, the children giggled and laughed. Marcus made up a song for them to sing.

When they reached Richmond, Elizabeth waved to several of the people she knew. Marcus stopped in front of Thompson McMahon's store and tied the horses to the hitching post. While their mother bought supplies, the children wandered around the store and looked at everything. When Elizabeth finished, she walked to the wagon with a bag of peppermint sticks in her hand. The boys helped Marcus carry the supplies to the wagon.

Their spirits were high when they headed home. It was not often that they had candy to eat. Two-year-old Billy managed to get his candy all over his face and in his hair.

It was almost dark when they arrived home. The children were tired but happy. It had been a wonderful day. From that day on, Churchill knew his mother was going to marry Marcus Harry.

One evening, after supper, Elizabeth announced she had decided it was time to add another room onto the house. Marcus and the boys began chopping logs for the walls of the new room. They tied ropes onto the logs, and the oxen then pulled the logs up to the side of the house.

It was hard work, but when finished it was a fine addition to the house.

Soon after the room was finished, Churchill sensed something was about to happen. One day his mother took extra care preparing a special meal. She baked a sweet potato pie and cooked one of the chickens. After the table was set, Elizabeth smoothed down her hair and slipped on her clean apron. She sent Liz out to pick some sunflowers to put on the table.

When the family sat down to eat, they looked at each other in surprise. What was the special occasion? Elizabeth only smiled when they questioned her. From the sparkle in her eyes, Churchill knew his mother was happy. When they had finished eating and Marcus had his cup of coffee, Elizabeth asked for their attention.

"Children," she said, looking from one to another, "Marcus and I have something to tell you."

"Oh! Is it a surprise?" Billy cried.

Marcus reached across to tousle Billy's black curls with his hand. "Not exactly. Tell me, how would you like for me to be your dad?" Billy's mouth flew open. Marcus rumpled his curls again. "Your mother and I are getting married!"

"Married?" Liz cried. As the shock wore off, the two younger children danced around the kitchen, laughing and singing. "Ma's getting married! Ma's getting married!"

Elizabeth waited to hear what her older sons would say. Churchill laughed and slapped Marcus on the back. "Well, it's about time!" Churchill turned to hug his mother, but James was already hugging her. The boys gave them their blessings.

When Mr. Randon heard the news, he insisted that the wedding be at his house. Elizabeth invited only her sister Harriet and her family, along with a few close friends. The ceremony was performed in front of the fireplace in the Randons' parlor. Refreshments were served on the porch. Elizabeth blushed like a schoolgirl when her niece told her that she was a beautiful bride.

With goodwill wishes and farewell kisses, the guests departed. On the way home, Elizabeth kept thinking, "From this day on, I will be known as Mrs. Marcus Harry!"

The couple had not been married long when Marcus brought home two workers to help in the fields. Churchill and James found they had free time on their hands. When they heard the dogs baying in the middle of the night, they could go hunting. They would grab their guns and race out the door to see what Thumper had treed. Often as not, the boys returned with a raccoon or two.

It was not long before Marcus and the family returned to David Randon's for another wedding. They found the parlor crowded with guests who had come to see Elizabeth's niece, Mary, and Mr. Randon's nephew, Thomas Newman, pronounced man and wife. On the way home from the party, Churchill shared some news with his family. Mr. Randon had asked if he and James would like to work with his hounds.

The boys soon learned that their neighbor was very particular about his dogs. Mr. Randon demanded gentleness yet discipline from those who handled the hounds. With their natural instinct to track a scent, the dogs often wandered far from home once they were out of their cages. Some hounds were better trackers than others. It was those dogs that Mr. Randon wanted to keep for his kennels. It was Churchill's job to locate those superior animals.

Although the boys worked only a few days each week, they kept strange hours. They were given a room at the back of the Randon house, and they were free to come and go.

One morning Churchill decided he would visit his cousin, Mary. Mr. Randon had given Thomas and Mary some land and a house of their own when they got married. When Churchill arrived at Mary's, she was bubbling with news. Thomas's younger sister and his mother, Elizabeth Newman, were moving to Texas from Alabama. They would stay with the Randons until a house could be built for them.

On the way home Churchill thought about Thomas's mother. What would she be like? After all, Mr. Randon was her brother. And Churchill thought David Randon was the greatest man in all the world.

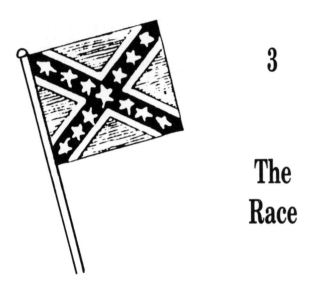

3

The Race

Before the year was over, Churchill had a baby sister. They named her Harriet. Since Billy was no longer the baby in the family, he wanted to grow up overnight. He pleaded to go fishing with the older boys. He begged Marcus to teach him how to ride a horse. However, his legs were much too short to reach the stirrups. Everyone teased Liz that she was growing like a weed. Churchill somehow felt life was moving too fast.

One afternoon Churchill and James were riding their horses to the Randons when they heard a scream.

"Whoa! Stop!"

Churchill scanned the countryside, trying to locate the sound.

"Stop! Whoa!"

"James — look! That girl's lost control of her horse!" Churchill rode swiftly through the grove of trees and out across the open field. He was less than fifty feet from the girl when her horse suddenly swerved. Caught completely by surprise, the girl let the reins slip through her fingers. She tumbled to the ground.

"Are you all right?" Churchill cried, racing to her side.

The girl sat up, rubbing her arm. She stared at him.

"Here, let me help you up. Are you hurt, little girl?"

She ignored his outstretched hand and got to her feet. "Of course I am. And I am not a little girl. I'm thirteen!" Her dark eyes flashed. She brushed the dirt from her skirt. From the twinkle in his eyes she felt the boy was laughing at her.

"Thirteen? You look much younger," he mumbled, looking around for her horse. When he saw it, he shook his head. "No wonder you fell — there's no saddle on that horse!"

"I know that!" she cried indignantly.

Churchill stared from the girl to the mare grazing calmly nearby. "You can't ride like that! Girls don't ride bareback!"

"Why not? My people . . ." She stopped. Her Uncle David had warned her to tell no one that she was an Indian. He said some people in Texas did not like Indians. Lifting her head proudly, her black eyes blazed. "My uncle said I could ride Rosy bareback if I wanted to! So there!"

Churchill rocked on his heels with a wide grin on his face. "So you are Mr. Randon's niece from Alabama?"

Susan Newman nodded, looking at him more closely. His dark hair and eyes blended well with his olive-colored skin. He seemed pleasant but there was something about his voice she did not like. She resented being treated like a child.

"What is your name, girl?"

"Stop calling me girl! My name is Elizabeth Susan Newman. Folks usually call me Susan."

Churchill chuckled softly. "That's good, because Elizabeth seems to be a popular name. I heard Mr. Randon speak of your mother as Elizabeth. That is also the

17

Churchill was not far from the girl when her horse swerved and she tumbled to the ground.

name of my mother and sister. But most people call my mother Betsy. My sister is called Liz. By the way, my name is Churchill Roberts. I'm your neighbor."

"And what are you doing on my uncle's land?" she demanded.

"I work for Mr. Randon sometimes. Say, would you like for me to take you home? After that fall you probably don't feel much like getting back on that horse. Rosy will find her way back by herself."

"No," Susan cried, "that horse has to learn I mean to ride her bareback!"

"But . . ."

Susan ran for the horse before he could finish. She grabbed the reins with one hand and Rosy's long mane with the other as she leaped upon the mare's back. Then she rode off toward the creek without a backward glance.

"Hey — wait for me!" Churchill shouted. He could have saved his breath. By the time he was on his horse, she was far ahead. He had never seen a girl ride as she was riding. She had her head pressed against the mare's neck and was tightly grasping its flowing mane. The wind was blowing Susan's long, black hair in all directions.

Churchill felt certain he could catch up with her before Susan crossed the creek. He was wrong. Susan's horse galloped through the shallow water, up the opposite bank, and on toward Thomas's house. Rosy raced into the yard and stopped under one of the large pecan trees. With a half-grin on her face, Susan slid to the ground to wait for Churchill.

Churchill was panting breathlessly when he rode up beside her. "Say, who taught you to ride like that?"

Susan shrugged her shoulders. She wanted to tell him that most Indian children learned to ride bareback at an early age, but she remembered her uncle's warning.

"I never saw a girl ride like that before," he said, wiping his brow. "I would like to race you again someday.

But we should start out together next time. Maybe I could win."

Susan's eyes danced with laughter. "Maybe. But before we race, Rosy must learn I mean business." With that, Susan abruptly turned and walked into the house.

In the days that followed, Susan had little time to think of Churchill. As soon as her chores were finished she spent her time training Rosy. The horse learned to respond to the touch of Susan's knees against her sides, the gentle tug on her mane, and the nudge of Susan's toes in her flank.

Susan never knew her Uncle David was watching her when she rode across the open field. He often muttered to himself, "That girl may move to Texas and change her name from Natura to Susan, but anyone can see she is an Indian through and through."

Susan's uncle was not the only one watching from a distance. Churchill watched her too. He had never seen anyone quite like her.

Late one afternoon, several months later, Susan stopped at Mill Creek to water her horse. She slipped to the ground and bent over to splash the cool water in her face. Churchill and his brothers were watching her from the opposite bank.

"Well, young lady, how are you today?" Churchill called.

Susan looked up in surprise. She somehow felt he was spying on her. "And what are you doing here?"

Churchill chuckled softly, waving his fishing pole from side to side. "We're fishing. Say, have you met my brothers, James and Billy?"

Susan glanced toward the boys and nodded. "And does my uncle know you are here?"

With his brothers listening, Churchill did not like her attitude. He decided to set her straight. "Young lady, someone ought to teach you some Texas manners! This water belongs to everybody. And this creek runs from our land down to here. I reckon you could say my brothers are helping me catch *our* fish to take them home."

Susan was startled by his tone.

Seeing the expression on her face, Churchill threw back his head and laughed. "Girl, you are about the friskiest critter I ever saw! You remind me of a treed wildcat the way you spit and hiss!" Churchill jumped to his feet as Susan turned to her horse. "Don't leave. I didn't mean to make you angry. I'm sorry. Won't you stay and talk?" He realized his words were useless as she leaped upon her horse. He shouted, "Say, when are we going to have that race? You promised, remember?"

Susan glanced over her shoulder. Her dark eyes sparkled with devilment. "Come on. I'll race you right now."

"James, you and Billy go on home without me," Churchill yelled, dropping his fishing pole. He raced for his horse, shouting, "Hey, Susan, remember we agreed to start out together. No fair cheating this time."

Rosy pawed the ground impatiently, waiting for Churchill to catch up. When the two horses were side by side, Susan yelled, "Let's go!" They were off!

Churchill's brothers jumped up and down yelling for Susan to win as the racers vanished behind the trees. The horses dashed up the creek bank, through the grove of trees, and on across the field. As Churchill let his horse have the reins it inched slowly ahead. Susan smiled and waited. When Churchill's white horse was a length ahead of hers, Susan touched Rosy in the flank with her toe. Her horse shot forward like a bullet. Churchill was left far behind.

Racing into the yard, Susan slid to the ground. She smiled smugly. "You see," she said when he rode up beside her, "I don't have to cheat to beat you."

Churchill grinned sheepishly. "I guess you are right. You did it again. This time you won fair and square too."

Susan pushed the wisps of damp hair from her eyes.

"Well, since that is settled, I reckon you ought to come on in and have a cup of coffee."

Churchill was surprised at the change in her. Susan was almost friendly after that. He became a regular visitor to her house. Susan and her mother enjoyed his visits. He was a good storyteller. He liked to tell the stories he had heard about life in early Texas. His mother was five years old and his father was ten when they came to Texas with their parents and Stephen Austin. He told them that David Randon had attended his parents' wedding in 1834.

Churchill also told them how Mexico's new president, General Santa Anna, had earlier passed laws the settlers did not like. When the settlers talked of freedom, Santa Anna had gathered an army to march through Texas. He told of his father fighting in the battle at the Alamo, known as the Siege of Bexar. Churchill's voice sank to a whisper as he told of some 189 Texans being killed at the Alamo on March 6, 1836. He was proud to tell how the Texans had defeated Santa Anna at the Battle of San Jacinto in less than twenty minutes.

Churchill always ended his stories by saying, "I am mighty proud to be a Texan."

After hearing his stories, Elizabeth Newman and her daughter were proud to be a part of Texas too.

4

War Begins!

Three years flew by. One afternoon David Randon was sitting on his porch talking to his sister and his niece. Sighing deeply, he shook his head. "Mark my word — there will be war, Elizabeth."

"But why?" Susan demanded.

"Child, the people of the North have always opposed slavery. I reckon that is understandable. Up north they do not have big plantations like we have in the South. They don't realize we need our workers. Without them, what would happen to our cotton and corn? Northerners seem to forget they need our products to run their factories. We send them goods to manufacture, then we buy them back. The way I see it, they need us and our workers. But everyone knows President Abraham Lincoln is against slavery." David sighed again. "Elizabeth, maybe I made a mistake three years ago insisting that you and Susan come to Texas."

"Now, David, they have been good years. You and

Nancy have been very kind to us. Susan Natura and I did not want to stay in Alabama after my husband died. If he had lived, James Algier would have come too. He knew I wanted to be near you and Thomas. Susan Natura missed her brother after he came to Texas." Elizabeth looked at her daughter.

David frowned. "Now, sister, I notice you are using Susan's Indian name, Natura. I have told you before that folks around here don't feel too kindly toward Indians."

"I just forgot." Susan's mother changed the subject. "Do you really think there will be a war?"

He nodded. "No doubt about it. The South has seceded from the Union. Now Jefferson Davis is president of the new government of the Confederate States of America. And Sam Houston has resigned as governor of Texas rather than sign an oath of allegiance to the Confederacy. And Texas has joined South Carolina, Mississippi, Alabama, Georgia, Florida, and Louisiana in leaving the Union. Yes, I am certain there will be war."

Grim-faced, Elizabeth stared at the floor.

Susan spoke up. "Churchill says some of the men here in Fort Bend County are forming a group of Minutemen. He says they would be ready in a moment's notice if there is trouble."

"David, how do you feel about war? Is it the answer?" Elizabeth asked.

"Well, as I see it, sister, we have no choice. However, I agree with those who say a war between the North and the South will be like brother fighting brother. It was different back in 1836 during the Texas Revolution. We were fighting for our freedom from Mexico." He rubbed his chin thoughtfully. "Elizabeth, if you had stayed in Alabama, you and Susan could have gone to our people. You would have been safe with our Indian brothers."

"But if we had not come to Texas I wouldn't have met Churchill!" Susan cried.

Her uncle smiled. He had watched the two young people and was surprised that it was Churchill, and not

24

his younger brother James, who was attracted to Susan. With war so near, he wondered what the future might hold for them. David Randon shook his head. "My dear, Churchill and James will probably both be in the army before this year is over. No doubt your brother will be joining too."

"Oh, Uncle David, don't say that!" Susan's eyes filled with tears. She ran from the porch around the corner of the house. She wanted to be alone. Under the big oak tree she sank to the ground and stared at the cloudless April sky. Susan's thoughts drifted back to the happy times she had shared with Churchill and his brothers. How could she have acted so childish and silly when she first met them? Why had she been so angry when Churchill called her a little girl? No wonder he called her a feisty wildcat. Susan hung her head. She admitted to herself she had acted like a child. But that was all over. They were friends now — good friends.

A gentle breeze rustled through the leaves. Susan remembered her uncle's words. She clinched her fist angrily. "War! I hate it! I hate it!"

Susan did not know then that the first shots had already been fired. It had happened far away at Fort Sumter, near Charleston, South Carolina, in the early morning darkness of April 12, 1861. The citizens of Charleston had stood by cheering for Brigadier General Pierre Beauregard and his Confederate soldiers as they poured more than 3,000 shells into the Union garrison. Two days later, Fort Sumter fell. The Civil War had started!

It was not long before everyone was talking of war. President Lincoln had called for 42,000 volunteers for the Union army.

With the news of the Battle of Bull Run, feelings ran high in Texas. The Yankees of the North and the Rebel army of the South had met on a small winding river known as Bull Run on July 21, 1861. The North had felt certain of victory at first when they forced the Confederate lines to move back. Suddenly, one of the Confederates shouted, "Look! There is Jackson standing like a stone wall!" The Virginians stared at their leader, Brigadier General Thomas Jackson.

For some unexplainable reason those words sparked the dying embers within the hearts of the Confederates. They rallied to the cause and turned like a swarm of angry bees around a hive of honey. The Union soldiers were stunned by the change in the Confederates. They turned on their heels to retreat.

Unfortunately, the people of Washington, D.C., had not taken the fighting seriously. Large numbers of them had packed picnic baskets and hitched up their carriages, wagons, and buggies to go out to watch the fighting. The buggies were crowded with stylish women wearing billowy dresses and distinguished men dressed in the latest fashions. As the picnickers neared the Bull Run River, the sound of their laughter and happy voices could be heard. Some were midway across the bridge over Bull Run River when the Union soldiers began retreating. The Northern troops ran headlong into the startled merrymakers. The bridge became jammed and impassable.

Suddenly, in the midst of the confusion, the Confederates turned their cannon on the bridge and fired. For an instant the bridge seemed to hang in midair over the river; then it split apart. Screams of pain and fear filled the air as the bridge sank into the water. Swimming for shore was impossible. The wagons and carriages, along with the billowy-skirted women clawing for help, blocked the way. Bull Run River became the watery grave for scores of men and women and animals that day.

The damages of that battle defied description. The North reported some 3,000 wounded or missing, with 2,000 casualties for the South. Rebels and Yankees were buried side by side in unmarked graves. Two Northern generals, William Sherman and George Custer, and Confederate General Robert E. Lee would long be remembered for their part in the Battle of Bull Run.

On Christmas Day, 1861, the tragedy of war touched

the Texans in Fort Bend County, Texas. They met at Oakland Plantation to pay their last respects to their lifelong friend, Colonel Frank Terry. They learned that at Woodsonville, Kentucky, on the Green River, the colonel had led his men into battle. With his cry, "Charge, my brave boys, charge!" Terry's Texas Rangers defeated the enemy. When the battle was over, his men found Colonel Terry among the dead.

With the news of the surrender of two Confederate forts — Fort Henry on the Tennessee River and Fort Donelson on the Cumberland River — spirits were low. Susan knew Churchill would soon be leaving to join the Confederate army. It was just a matter of time. About 2,000 Texans had already volunteered. Others were preparing to leave. Most were concerned about their fields of sugar cane and corn. The cotton would soon be ready for picking. How would the women and children and men who were too old to fight be able to harvest the crops?

Susan had heard Churchill talking to James and Thomas about joining Terry's Rangers. They had decided to wait. Like others in Texas, they had mixed feelings about the war. They agreed with Sam Houston. There must be a better way to settle the differences between the North and South. In the spring of 1862 the Confederate government of the Southern states voted to draft men to serve in the army.

One warm afternoon in May, Susan heard Churchill calling her name. "Hey, Sue, I want to talk to you!"

Susan and her mother hurried out onto the porch. "What is it, boy?" Elizabeth Newman demanded. "What is wrong?"

"Ma'am, I have come to say goodbye. My brother James and I are joining Edwin Waller's regiment. Would you mind if Susan rode down to the creek with me? I would like to talk to her before I leave."

"Of course not. You two run along."

"Wait until I get my horse," Susan cried. "I'll be right with you."

27

"No, Sue, I haven't time. Give me your hand. You can ride with me. We won't be gone long. James is waiting for me."

After she was seated, Churchill wheeled his horse around. Susan grabbed onto his shirt to keep from falling. She was not used to riding a horse like that. When they reached the creek, Churchill jumped to the ground to help her down. They sat on an old, dead tree to talk. Susan waited for Churchill to speak. His first words were not what she expected.

"Sue, I brought you here for a reason. I have something to say. Did I tell you this is the spot where my mother and father used to come before they were married?" He clasped Susan's hand tightly. "I know this is sudden, but I can't go away without telling you." He paused.

"Yes? What is it, Churchill?"

"I guess I have always thought of you as if you were a little sister. Now that I'm going away I know you are more than that. You have a special place in my heart. Sue," he kissed her fingertips, "I love you!" Her soft brown eyes, her high cheekbones, her long, black hair and slender body were impressed upon his mind. Churchill knew he would carry a picture of her in his heart forever. "Will you marry me if I come back from the war?"

"Oh, Churchill," her eyes filled with tears, "don't say *if* you come back, but *when* you come back. But . . . I can't marry you."

"Why not? I love you, and I hoped that you might feel the same toward me."

"Before you say any more, I must tell you . . ." her brown eyes lowered. "I can't marry you because . . . because I am an Indian! I wanted to tell you but Uncle David forbade me to tell anyone."

"Don't cry," Churchill said, brushing a tear from her eye. "I know you have Indian blood in you. Your brother told me. But don't you see? It doesn't matter to me one bit! I love you! Now will you marry me?"

"Oh, yes, I will! I would marry you today if you wanted me to. I love you so much!"

He gently took her in his arms. They had no need for further words.

Susan felt her heart had wings as they rode home. She was surprised to see her brother and his wife along with Uncle David in the yard talking to her mother. As Churchill helped her from his horse, Susan sensed something was wrong. "What is it, Mother?"

"Well," her mother said grimly, "looks like all of our boys are leaving. Thomas is joining Colonel Waller's regiment along with Churchill."

"Now, Mother," Thomas said, patting his mother's hand, "you know I talked about joining Terry's Texas Rangers last year when he recruited others from Fort Bend County. A great number of our neighbors are already fighting in this war. I feel it is my duty to go. Mary agrees with me, don't you, honey?"

"Thomas is right, Mother Newman. The South needs help," Mary said.

Churchill nodded. "I reckon we are needed. Colonel Waller told us to bring our guns and horses along with a bridle, blanket, saddle, and lariat rope. Sounds like there is a shortage of equipment if we have to bring our own. By the way, Mrs. Newman," Churchill grinned sheepishly, "I reckon you ought to know I asked your daughter to marry me when I get home from the war. That is, if we have your permission."

Susan's brother slapped Churchill on the back. "Congratulations!"

A pleased smile crossed the older woman's face. "You two have my blessings. You will make Susan a fine husband, son."

"Thank you, ma'am. I will try."

"James will be wondering what has happened to us. I reckon we had better be going." Thomas looked at his uncle. "I know you will watch after Mother and my sister.

Would you keep an eye on Mary and my son, Uncle David?"

"Don't worry about the womenfolk, boys. I will see they are cared for. And Churchill, tell your brother I am mighty proud to be watching after your dogs while you boys are gone. It is the least I can do." David Randon shook hands with Churchill and then Thomas. "I only regret I am too old to go with you. You boys take care of yourselves. Hurry back."

Thomas hugged his mother and sister fondly. With his son in one arm and his other arm around his wife, he said, "Be a good boy, Algier. Mind your Ma."

"I'll be good, Pa," the four-year-old promised.

Churchill took Susan in his arms for one last kiss. He whispered tenderly, "Wait for me, Sue. I will be back."

With words of encouragement and final farewells, the two mounted their horses and rode away in silence.

Churchill wondered what might lie ahead. Gazing into the clear blue sky, he muttered a prayer. "Let this war be over soon — please."

Churchill and his two companions rode off to war.

5

Off to Fight

On the following day, Churchill and his two companions rode into the town square of Hempstead. There they joined other volunteers who were awaiting orders. A short time later, a bearded soldier rode up, looked the men over, and ordered, "You recruits mount up and follow me!"

Thomas and the two Roberts brothers trailed behind the other volunteers as the soldier rode out of town, south toward Camp Waller. As they entered the camp, Churchill saw Jack Stafford and several of the other men that he knew from Fort Bend County.

"You fellows unsaddle your horses and turn them out to graze with those others over there. Put your gear over yonder and make yourselves at home," announced the bearded soldier who had brought them to Camp Waller.

"Hey, mister! When do we get our uniforms?" one of the young recruits demanded.

"Uniforms?" the bearded fellow roared. "You're wearing them. You're lucky if ya get salt pork and coffee without expectin' a uniform too."

Churchill frowned. He hoped the rest of the men were more friendly than this one.

"Leapin' lizards," someone moaned. "Here comes Sergeant Lacey. That means we're gonna march."

And march they did — for hours! Churchill wondered if the sergeant would ever stop. Churchill never knew that his feet could be so tired. He could hardly walk, but he had no trouble sleeping that night.

The next day was Sunday. Churchill attended the preaching service with the others. That afternoon the sergeant ordered them to line up for inspection. Churchill noticed that most of the guns passed the inspection. The men already knew that a clean gun could mean the difference between life and death.

"I'm gonna make soldiers out of you recruits yet," Sergeant Lacey growled. "Come on — pick up your feet. Left, right, left, right." They drilled and drilled for hours.

On the evening of June 27 the sergeant shouted, "You fellows stand at attention. We're having a dress parade." When it was over, even the sergeant agreed it was quite a show.

After the parade, someone said that the group would be moving very soon. It was rumored that they were going to a place in Louisiana called New Iberia.

Spirits were high as the group rode out of Camp Waller on July 1. They made camp that night at Clear Creek. Churchill was grateful there was plenty of grass for the horses. During the days that followed, the battalion journeyed in a southeasterly direction toward Louisiana. The roads were dry and dusty. Before the week was over, it began to rain. The roads were soon muddy and hard to travel. Several of the supply wagons broke down and were left behind for repairs.

Most of the people that the soldiers met along the way were friendly. They insisted that the men help themselves to watermelons growing in their fields. After a long day the watermelons tasted mighty good. On some days the group traveled six or seven miles. At other times they rode twenty or more miles before stopping for the night. They found the town of Livingston deserted. Someone said they were not far from the Louisiana border.

Churchill was interested in the countryside. At some places there might be plenty of good water but no grass for the horses. At the next stop there was plenty of corn and fodder for the animals but the water would be too bitter to drink. Churchill saw few men in the towns along the way. He guessed that the able-bodied ones had joined the army.

The flat black land changed to reddish brown hills. The mules had trouble pulling the heavy wagons as the roads grew worse. Travel slowed to a snail's pace. Someone said they were not far from the Neches River. That river was wide and deep. Churchill wondered how they would ever get the supply wagons across. It was quite simple. The wagons were loaded onto a flat ferryboat and pulled across the river. The men had trouble getting the wagons up the slippery bank on the opposite side. A short distance from the river it began to rain. When the battalion stopped for the night, they discovered that the tents were in the wagons they had left behind.

"I ain't never been so wet," one fellow grumbled.

"Aw, stop complainin'," another said. "We can use a bath."

The next morning they were unable to travel because of the mud. The men busied themselves washing their clothes and cleaning their guns.

"Just look at us. We don't look much like Confederate soldiers," Churchill chuckled as he glanced at his buddies. Most of the men wore homespun shirts, tattered pants, and sloppy black felt hats. The first Confederate soldiers had been issued light blue trousers and gray jackets when they joined the army. The trimming on the hats indicated whether they were in the infantry, cavalry, or artillery. Before the war, most of the ready-made clothing came from factories in the North. Money and cloth were now scarce. The South could no longer supply uniforms for the soldiers. Churchill was right! They did not look much like soldiers.

Thomas nodded. "We may not look like soldiers, but did you ever see so many revolvers, shotguns, carbines, and muskets? And just look at all the bowie knives. Why, some must be three feet long! If I saw one of those knives coming at me I would sure tremble. I'll bet the Yankees will too."

"Someone said the captain counted the number of firearms in our battalion," James said. "He counted forty-eight shotguns, thirty-nine six-shooters, and a number of regular rifles, as well as some saber rifles. When we get more men, that number will go up. I reckon that ought to scare those Yankees, don't you?"

Before the week was over, they reached the Sabine River. That river was the boundary between Texas and Louisiana. The men weren't happy to find that the small ferryboat which serviced the river could carry only one wagon at a time. They had to help pole the boat across. It was slow work.

That night Colonel Waller said, "Men, our supplies are getting low. The bacon is not fit to eat. And you are drinking the last of the coffee until our supplies get here." Everyone groaned.

The next morning a number of the men were sick. They had to be left behind until they were able to travel again.

A few evenings later, Colonel Waller called the men together. He raised his hand for silence. "Soldiers," he began, "we will stay here at Camp Texas for a while. There is plenty of grass and water for the animals. We are not far from La Fayette and New Iberia. This will be a fine camp once our supply wagons and other equipment catch up with us."

The colonel neglected to tell the men that it would

probably rain every day. Churchill figured that was why the grass, trees, and bushes were so thick and green.

The battalion had been in Camp Texas a few days when someone brought the mail. Thomas received a letter from his wife. Churchill was disappointed he did not receive one from Susan.

"Have you written to my sister?" Thomas asked. Churchill hung his head. "Well, Mother won't let Susan write to you until you write her. I'll give you some paper."

With paper and pen in hand, Churchill leaned against a tree to compose a letter.

August 5, 1862
at Camp Texas

Dear Susan,

We are somewhere near a place called La Fayette in Louisiana. We have been here almost a week. We are fine. James is disappointed because we haven't seen any Yankees yet. I guess we will be seeing them before long. Some of the boys are sick with a fever. It rains almost every day. That may be why they are sick. The people around here are very kind. I have trouble understanding the way they talk. Someone said they are French and that is why their accent is different. Colonel Waller said we would stay here for a while. I sure would like to get a letter from you. Some of the fellows got mail today, but there was none for me. I sure hope this war is over in a hurry. I want to come home to you. Tell your mother hello for James and me. If you see my mother, tell her I love her too.

Your friend,
Churchill

P.S. Tell your uncle hello.

Churchill looked at the letter and shook his head.

There was so much he wanted to say. He was afraid of how it might sound if he put it on paper. He decided he would wait until he had a letter from Susan before he told her what was in his heart. When he folded the letter Churchill had a terrible thought. What if Susan had changed her mind about marrying him?

6

The Swamp Battle

"Men, as your commander," Colonel Waller said, "I want you to know that I expect this Thirteenth Texas Cavalry Battalion to be the best unit in the Texas Mounted Riflemen. How many of you agree this will be the best outfit in the Confederate army?" The colonel stared into the faces of his men. They cheered loudly.

"That's the spirit! Now . . ." he paused until a hush fell upon the group, "we have orders to move down the Mississippi River and capture Butte Station, which the enemy is holding. General Platt is in charge of a large force of Louisiana state militia. His troops will meet us at Butte Station. We hope to make a surprise attack on the Yankees. With luck we will take the railroad station. So saddle up! We are moving out!"

Waller's battalion quickly assembled and rode out of camp. The high-spirited men were eager for action. They were certain they could wipe out the enemy without any trouble. But their excitement quickly vanished when travel through the muddy swamps and tall sugar cane became difficult. It was impossible to get the heavy supply wagons through the marshes. The wagons had to be left behind.

The men made camp that night near a sugar mill owned by a man named Pane. Churchill and his comrades were unhappy to learn that their food supply was back in the wagons. They had nothing to eat. When the owner of the mill heard they were hungry, he told them to help themselves to the fruit on his trees. The soldiers ate their fill of figs and oranges and sugar cane. They decided to call the place Camp Pane.

The next morning the group rode on to Butte Station. They were disappointed to find that the town had been burned to the ground and was deserted. Not even a dog or chicken was in sight. Hopes of capturing a supply train and the railroad station vanished. Most of the railroad tracks had been pulled out of the ground. It would be impossible for a train to travel on them until repairs were made.

Colonel Waller told his men, "It will soon be dark. We'll return to Camp Pane and make camp."

Churchill and his buddies turned their horses around to retrace their steps. They were not far from the river. Suddenly, shortly after midnight, someone spotted three boats moving up the river. The two boats nearest the bank were loaded with Union soldiers. The other was a gunboat. Colonel Waller signaled his men to stop. They watched the soldiers pouring onto the bank from one of the ships.

"Men," Colonel Waller whispered loudly, "prepare for battle." The words were scarcely spoken when the enemy gunboat opened fire. Shells whizzed all around them. Waller's men were caught in a crossfire between the gunboat and the Union soldiers who had landed on the river bank. They could not stay where they were, and were forced to retreat into the swamp.

Colonel Waller headed into the marsh. His men were

right behind him. They soon found that their horses bogged down in the soft, knee-deep mud. The colonel said, "We seem to have no choice but to dismount and leave our horses behind. We can only try to get out of here on foot. Pass the word along."

"What about our equipment and blankets?" the sergeant demanded.

"We will leave those and come back for them and the horses tomorrow," the colonel said as he dismounted from his horse. The men followed his example.

Without a moon, the night was dark. There was nothing to light the way. The colonel and his battalion stumbled deeper and deeper into the swamp. They had escaped the Union soldiers only to be lost in the boggy marsh. Great masses of moss draped the branches of the trees and blotted out the sky.

The group zigzagged back and forth. Churchill felt that they were going in circles. By daybreak they were hopelessly lost, not knowing in which direction to go. The day wore on. To make matters worse, the mosquitoes swarmed around them. The men grumbled and complained. The sun was sinking in the west when one of the scouts chanced upon a clearing, and the unit wasted no time getting out of the marsh.

After they were on solid footing, the soldiers sank to the ground. Churchill stared at his comrades. They were wet and tired and hungry — truly a sad-looking bunch. Some had lost their shoes and hats in the swamp. Churchill shook his head. He remembered the excitement that day when they left Texas. No one was excited now.

"We will rest here for a while," Colonel Waller said.

Later, the colonel realized that was a mistake. While they were resting, the enemy somehow found their horses and equipment and loaded it onto their boats. The Yankees also managed to capture fifteen Confederate soldiers.

Churchill and the other soldiers were disgusted to

learn that not only were their horses stolen, but also their guns and supplies. Only a few of the group still had their horses. The others were forced to walk. Those without shoes were soon complaining bitterly. Their feet were killing them, for they were not used to walking barefoot. Yet without their horses, the cavalrymen were forced to become foot soldiers. Churchill and his comrades would never forget that experience.

While they waited for horses and supplies to come from Texas, the men grumbled about the food and the weather. One evening Churchill was talking to James and some of the others in his group. James said, "When I get back to Texas, I'll never again complain about the weather. Texas may be hot, but at least it's dry. If it isn't drizzling here, it's raining. And there is always a chill in this air."

"That's the truth, boy," a bearded man named Elisha Gray agreed. "I hate sloshing through these muddy swamps."

Thomas spoke up. "It is sleeping on the wet, soggy ground that I hate. Oh, for a nice dry bed. I wrote my wife that I'm too old for this soldier's life."

"I'm not as old as I feel these days," Churchill chuckled, looking at the new recruits. Some were only sixteen — too young to shave. A few were so green they did not know how to load or shoot a gun. Churchill thought of his younger brother back home. He prayed Billy would have enough sense to join the home guard so he could stay in Fort Bend County with the family.

Every few days, someone rode into Camp Texas with news of the war. They told stories of Generals Stonewall Jackson, Robert E. Lee, and Braxton Bragg, the commander of the Confederate Army of Mississippi. They told of battles in faraway places. They told of the Battle of Manassas in August 1862. In that three-day battle some 25,000 men had been killed. There were other battles, like the one at Savage Station on the Potomac River in Virginia. In the Seven Days' Battle there, at the end of

41

June, General Lee lost some 20,000 Confederate soldiers. Stories like those did little to lift Churchill's spirits.

Wounded soldiers on their way home sometimes stopped at Camp Texas. If any happened to be going near Fort Bend County, Churchill and Thomas would write letters for them to take with them. With luck, those letters eventually found their way to the right people. Soldiers rejoining their units often carried messages from families back home. This mail service was slow, but it was usually effective.

Churchill was interested in the stories about battles in distant places. He was particularly interested in stories about the Union army. The soldiers in the North and South seemed to have much in common. Their diet consisted of hardtack bread, salt pork, and coffee. It was comforting to know the Yankees were often hungry too. After months of battle, clothing had become worn and threadbare. Many Yankees felt the Rebels were the most ragged, lean, hungry bunch of men they had ever seen. It was true the Rebels were unshaven and shabby-looking. It was not surprising the Northerners thought that the Rebels looked frightening.

The animals suffered too. A number of horses and mules had already died of exhaustion or starvation.

Disease among the soldiers in both armies was a constant threat. Large numbers of men had come down with typhoid fever, malaria, and pneumonia. Churchill wondered if the bitter-tasting water they were forced to drink had made them sick.

There were stories of women helping the sick and dying with no thought about which side they were on. The crowded hospitals in Atlanta, Chattanooga, and Washington needed the women to roll bandages and care for the wounded.

One evening after riding patrol for hours, the men sat and talked around the campfire. Thomas said, "This war cannot be over soon enough for me. If we aren't on patrol, we are marching. I am no foot soldier."

Churchill nodded. "I would rather ride a horse any day than walk."

"May the good Lord deliver me from being a foot soldier in the infantry," Elisha Gray moaned. "Marching through the mud and swamps, up one hill and down another, is not for me."

"Yep," James agreed. "And fighting elbow to elbow the way those infantrymen do to protect each other from injury looks mighty dangerous. I'm glad we are in the cavalry."

"The Yankees will have a fight on their hands if they try to take my horse and gun again," Churchill declared grimly. He, like most of his comrades, was an expert marksman.

Thomas chuckled softly, "I wouldn't want to be in the artillery, either. Those fellows have to pull the smaller cannons. I understand those are heavy and hard to load. Some explode when they are fired. I reckon being in this outfit riding a horse is the best place for me if I have to be in the army."

There was a faraway look in Churchill's eyes. He muttered, "I would rather be home with Susan."

A hush fell upon the group. They thought of home and the loved ones they had left behind. Someone began to sing "The Yellow Rose of Texas." The others joined in. That song was followed by "Just Before the Battle, Mother" and "Old Abe, the Battle Eagle." Churchill was sad when they sang "Aura Lee" and "Lorena." Those songs reminded him of Susan. He longed for the day when he could return to Fort Bend County and make her his wife.

One evening the men talked about stories of the overcrowded prison camps. Someone said the prisoners were given a pint of coarse cornmeal and a tablespoon of peas a day. With so little to eat, it was no wonder so many soldiers died in the prisons.

"I would rather die than be put in one of those

places," Churchill said, staring into the campfire. "There are some things worse than death."

Thomas nodded. "War seems to bring out the worst in men. Some become cruel and heartless."

Later, when they were alone, Churchill looked from Thomas to his brother. "Let's make an agreement — just the three of us. No matter what happens, we will try to look after each other. Mother would never forgive me, James, if you got hurt. And no telling what Susan would do if we went home without you, Thomas. I don't want to think about it."

The three promised to watch out for each other. Thomas said, "War may bring out the worst in other men, but we can stick together."

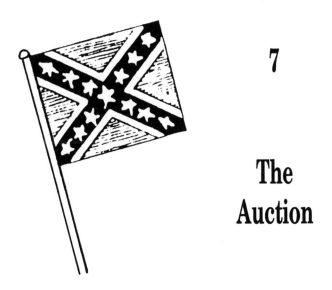

7

The
Auction

"Mercy, it's so hot," Susan grumbled, pushing the wisps of damp hair from her forehead. She leaned against her hoe to rest. Patches of fluffy clouds floated across the sky like soft white balls of cotton. Susan moaned at the thought of cotton. Hoeing was hot, hard work. Picking cotton was even harder.

With most of the able-bodied men away in the army, the women and children had to work in the fields. Everyone in Texas had been urged to grow more rice and corn to feed the soldiers. More cotton was also needed to make uniforms.

Union troops had blockaded a number of Southern ports. This meant that supply ships from Europe could no longer enter or leave those ports. The people of the South had trouble getting supplies. Susan's uncle often said that the Texans would never let the Union blockade all of the Texas ports. Susan hoped he was right.

"Mother, look at the blisters on my hands. I wonder

45

spected her husband's widowed sister. She had forsaken her Indian life when she had married James Algier Newman. She never spoke of her father, Chief Peter Randon, or her Creek Indian family back in Alabama. Elizabeth seemed content to be in Texas.

"Oh, Mother, can we go? Please?"

As Susan spoke, Nancy studied her niece. The toes of Susan's homemade moccasins peaked from beneath the hem of her faded homespun skirt. Her hair was plaited into two braids which hung down her back. Susan would make Churchill a beautiful wife.

"When is this auction?" Elizabeth asked. "We still have corn to pick."

"Oh, that old corn can wait," Nancy scolded. "The auction is this Saturday and everyone is going. We have been asked to take something to sell. David and I are taking fried chicken and some of my mustang grape jelly. Our neighbor, Hanny Perry, is making a cake. The Simontons are donating a bushel of sweet potatoes. Some of the women are making things. Money is scarce, but David thinks everybody can bring something to raise money for the soldiers' wives. Some families are having a mighty hard time. It is bad enough for their husbands to be off fighting without being worried about money."

"Oh, Mother, let's go," Susan pleaded. "You remember the honey I found in that bee tree? We could use that along with the rest of those pecans and make a pecan pie or two. Can't we go? Please. We never go anywhere."

Elizabeth sighed as she threw up her hands. "All right. We'll go."

That Saturday was one the folks of Fort Bend County would long remember. The people gathered in the Methodist Church at Richmond. Everyone stood around in groups, talking. They agreed that life was miserable with the men and boys away at war. Before the auction started, Susan and the others crowded around the tables in front of the room. Susan was amazed at the number and kinds of things to be sold. One lady had

48

made a number of billed caps. She had dyed them yellow with hickory bark. Someone said the cavalry soldiers wore billed caps like those when they were not wearing their black felt hats. Susan wished she could get one of those for Churchill. Some of the ladies had knitted socks and sweaters. There were also handmade shirts and trousers for sale. Everyone wanted those.

The people hurried to their seats as the preacher banged on the table to start the meeting. When everyone was quiet, the preacher told a joke and sang a funny song. Everyone laughed. There was excitement in the air when David Randon stepped forward to be the auctioneer. His dark eyes sparkled with merriment as he put on one of the yellow caps and danced around asking for bids. Susan was pleased when her mother bought a shirt for Thomas and a pair of socks for Susan to send to Churchill. Susan looked up in time to see Churchill's family come in and sit down.

When the auction was over, $460 had been raised. Everyone was amazed and pleased. They agreed to have another sale to raise money for the Confederate army. The preacher prayed for peace as the meeting ended. Susan waved to Churchill's mother when she started out the door. The people went home proud about what they had done that day.

The month of September was as hot and dry as the whole summer had been. The farmers needed rain.

The day that Churchill's letter arrived, Susan's hands trembled as she opened it. She scanned the page quickly, then read and reread it until she knew every word by heart. She went around the house smiling and humming the last line: "If you see my mother, tell her I love her too."

Susan wanted to answer the letter immediately, but she decided to visit Churchill's mother first. Susan's mother agreed that might be best. The next morning, Susan braided her hair with extra care and put on her clean dress. "Do I look all right, Mother?"

"You look fine, child. I have always heard 'beauty is as beauty does.' Run along now, but don't be too long. There is work to do." With loving eyes, Elizabeth watched her daughter ride off toward the home of Marcus and Elizabeth Harry.

Churchill's younger half sisters, Amanda and Sarah, were playing in the yard when Susan rode up. "Mama, Mama, we have company," Amanda cried.

Churchill's mother and little Harriet ran out to see who it might be. "Why, Susan! How good it is to see you. Do come in the house." With so much work and three small children, Churchill's mother had little time to go visiting.

Susan studied the family closely as they sat around the table. The three girls all talked at once about the snake their father had killed down by the creek. The girls had their mother's piercing blue eyes, which matched their fair skin and blondish curls. Churchill's younger brother, Billy, looked much like James and Churchill. The boy had quit chopping wood to go into the house to visit with Susan. He sat on the hearth, petting the fat black cat, while the others talked.

Susan turned her attention to Elizabeth Roberts Harry. Elizabeth insisted that Susan call her Betsy. Susan found it hard to believe that Betsy was almost her own mother's age. The two women were so different. Betsy seemed so young, but Susan knew she was in her early forties. Even in her homemade dress, Betsy was a handsome woman.

Comparing the two women, Susan thought about her mother. Like most Indian women, Elizabeth Newman had black hair and eyes. Her face was usually expressionless. She seldom smiled. Susan loved her mother dearly, but there was something special about Churchill's mother. She was like a breath of spring on a cold winter's day. Betsy radiated joy and happiness.

Susan wished she could stay longer, but she knew she must get home. Everyone — but Billy — kissed her goodbye. He shook her hand and made her promise to come again.

That night Susan sat down to write her letter.

Dear Churchill,

I wanted to answer your letter the minute it came, but I made myself wait until I visited your family. They are fine and send their love. Your mother is so pretty.

My mother and I are working hard. We almost have the field ready to plant the fall crop of corn. We need rain. We went to an auction in Richmond with Uncle David. I made two pecan pies to sell. My mother bought Thomas a shirt and a pair of socks for you. Your mother is sending you and James some things. I will give her the socks. I hope you get them.

Please write again real soon. Will you please tell my brother that I love him too?

Your loving friend,
Susan

Susan sealed the letter with a kiss. There was no way Churchill would ever know. She wore no color on her lips.

Susan was amazed at how quickly bad news could travel. They heard that Union ships had captured the city of Galveston in October. Susan knew Galveston was one of Texas's busiest seaports. She had heard her uncle talk of how important all the ports along the coast and the border were to Texas. Those ports were needed to ship supplies to the Confederate soldiers. Susan felt uneasy knowing that the enemy troops were less than a hundred miles away.

General John Magruder was soon made the commander of Confederate forces in Texas. It was rumored that the general had a daring plan for retaking Galveston. Early in the morning darkness of January 1, 1863, the general made his move. The decks of two riverboats — the *Bayou City* and the *Neptune* — were piled high with bales of cotton for protection against the enemy shells. The ships sailed down Buffalo Bayou from Houston toward the Union ships anchored in Galveston harbor. The Union forces, sleeping soundly, were caught completely by surprise. During the attack two Union gunboats were destroyed. The other gunboats escaped. Before the battle was over, several hundred Union soldiers and their commander had surrendered. News that Galveston was once more in Confederate hands spread quickly. Susan heaved a sigh of relief.

8

"Keep firing, men!"

While General Magruder's forces were retaking Galveston, Churchill's battalion was preparing for battle in Louisiana. The enemy was reportedly planning to cross Berwick Bay in troop ships and move toward the Confederate headquarters at Alexandria, Louisiana. Colonel Waller's battalion was assigned to General Thomas Green's command and was ordered to stop the Union forces.

The town of Berwick was on the opposite side of the bay from the Union forces. Colonel Waller posted several of his men in an old frame building at the edge of Berwick. From there they could report on the enemy's movements.

On the morning of April 11, 1863, the Union ships came into view, carrying some 7,000 soldiers. Churchill's unit was ordered to move into place behind a high embankment. His heart beat fast as he watched the enemy soldiers disembark from the ships. They formed their battle positions to the beat of their drums with banners flying. The Confederates did not move until the Union troops were within shooting range; then they opened fire. Colonel Waller shouted above the noise, "Keep firing, men, but hold your position!"

Again and again the enemy tried to move forward. Again and again the Confederates turned them back. The Union soldiers were forced to retreat. The Confederates fought bravely, but when the battle was over, they learned they had lost their gunboat — the *Diana*. That ship had been captured from the enemy, after a brief battle, a few weeks earlier. But everyone agreed that it was "easy come, easy go" in time of war.

Colonel Waller's battalion met the enemy again on May 20 at Cheneyville, Louisiana. Churchill and his buddies took up their position behind a row of tall bushes. They hoped to ambush the Union soldiers, who were reportedly heading their way. The colonel sent a small detachment on ahead to act as decoys to lure the enemy into position.

"James . . . Thomas . . . listen," Churchill whispered hoarsely. "I hear their bugles sounding 'boots and saddles.' That means they are mounting their horses to chase our boys. Get ready! The Yankees are coming!"

Churchill was right. They soon heard the sound of horses galloping in their direction. Suddenly, the Confederates dashed into view. About seventy-five Union soldiers were right behind.

"Wait until our men are in the clear, then open fire," the colonel ordered.

The scene soon became one of confusion, with shooting, yelling, and the slashing of sabers. The Union soldiers quickly realized they were outnumbered. They wheeled their horses around to retreat. The Confederates managed to capture twenty of the enemy in the brief battle.

Later, Colonel Waller told his men: "You did a fine job in that ambush at Cheneyville last month. We are now planning a sneak attack on the enemy at Fort Buch-

anan. I think most of you know Major Sherod Hunter."
He pointed to the man beside him.

"Hunter's a good man," someone whispered loudly.

"The major needs fifty volunteers to go with him. Which of you will go with the major?" asked the colonel.

Thomas Newman and the two Roberts boys were among the first to step forward. The major motioned for them to follow him. He told the volunteers they were to cross the swamps of Grand Lake in small boats during the night. The next morning they would sneak up behind the enemy, after General Green's regiment opened fire. Churchill thought it sounded like a good plan at first. Unfortunately, they had problems. In the dark of the night, the volunteers could not see where they were going. They were unable to land the boats for the reeds and cattails growing in the water. They had to leave the boats and walk in water up to their knees to get to land.

At daybreak the next morning, General Green and his men surprised the enemy. The battle had already started when Major Hunter's volunteers arrived. With wild yells and bayonets fixed, the major and his mud-spattered men ran out of the woods to join in the fight. Churchill was with those who dashed ahead to climb the walls of Fort Buchanan. They tore down the Union flag to raise their own. Victory was theirs in less than twenty minutes. The Confederates captured eleven siege guns and thousands of smaller weapons. They took 2,000 horses and mules along with 1,300 prisoners.

When the battle was over, Churchill muttered to himself, "Some of these Yankees are too young to be called men. They aren't much older than Billy." He looked at one of the prisoners and thought of his younger brother. "I pray this war will be over soon. It seems so foolish."

A short distance from Fort Buchanan, Union forces attacked the Confederates at Fort Hudson, Louisiana. The fort surrendered in July. The surrender of this fort gave the Union control of the Mississippi River.

During the spring of 1863, there were a number of fierce battles between the North and the South. Wounded soldiers returning home reported on those battles. Churchill lost count of the number of victories and defeats. Both sides were suffering heavy losses.

There were stories of General Ulysses Grant's first engagement against the South at Vicksburg, Mississippi. In that siege on May 1, some 130 Union soldiers were killed and 718 were wounded. The Confederates lost half that number. Word came that 30,000 Confederate troops surrendered to General Grant on July 4. That news upset Churchill and his comrades.

They heard of other battles in distant places. At Chancellorsville, Virginia, General Joseph Hooker led his Union forces against General Robert E. Lee and General Stonewall Jackson on the first of May. News of the losses during the four-day battle was sobering. The numbers ran into the thousands.

The South had lost one of its finest generals — Stonewall Jackson. The general had been accidentally shot by one of his own men. Churchill and the others mourned his death.

"James, the price of war can never be measured in dollars and cents," Churchill said solemnly. "At the rate we are killing each other, I wonder how many men will be left alive to go home when this war is over."

His brother sighed. "I just hope Billy stays home."

Spirits rose when the men heard of the Battle of Chickamauga in northern Georgia. In September 1863 the Confederates had defeated the Union forces. Someone said "Chickamauga" was a Cherokee word which meant "river of death." The river had been red with blood when the Battle of Chickamauga had ended. Churchill shook his head as he heard the others talking. He was thinking of the number of mothers whose sons would never be coming home. No amount of tears could ever bring them back.

Things in Texas were quiet after General Magruder

took Galveston from the Yankees. But the quiet would not last long. On September 8, 1863, twenty-two Union transport ships and four gunboats sailed from New Orleans. They were on their way to the southeastern coast of Texas. They sailed into Sabine Pass — some sixty miles up the coast from Galveston. The Union commander planned to land near the pass and march his men overland to capture the cities of Beaumont and Houston. The commander did not know that six cannons and a company of forty-seven men were guarding the pass. Lieutenant Dick Dowling was the Confederate commander in charge of Sabine Pass. His men were called the Davis Guards.

The Union commander wanted to sail his ships silently by the pass without being detected. His plan did not work. The Davis Guards were waiting. When the ships were within range, the Confederates opened fire. They managed to disable two gunboats and to take 350 prisoners. The other Union vessels escaped and returned to New Orleans. Although the battle was brief, the lieutenant and his Guards had turned back the enemy. Their bravery gave hope to the people of Texas.

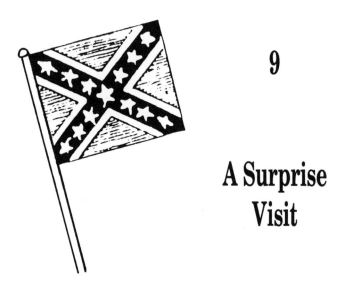

9

A Surprise
Visit

While the people in Texas were cheering for the Davis Guards, Churchill's group was fighting in western Louisiana. One evening, after days of hit-and-run attacks against the Union forces, the men of Company D had a chance to sit and rest. Churchill looked from his brother to his comrades and shook his head. "Tell me — do you have trouble remembering where we have been? I cannot recall all the battles we've fought or even where we have been!"

"That's true," Elisha Gray said, scratching his head thoughtfully. "I remember the battles at Sterling's Plantation, Camp Pratt, Buzzard's Prairie, and — of course — here at Morgan's Point. But the other places sort of run together in my head."

Thomas chuckled grimly. "Some of those places I want to forget."

Elisha Gray peered over his shoulder to make certain none of the officers were within hearing distance. He whispered loudly, "I overheard General Green talking. He said that the Yankees under General Banks have invaded Texas at several points along the coast."

"What? Invaded Texas? Gray, are you sure?" Thomas demanded excitedly.

Private Gray nodded. "That's not all." He leaned closer to the group, lowering his voice. "I heard the general say he's expecting orders from the commander of the District of Texas — General John Magruder — for our division to return to Texas!" The men looked at each other in surprise. Everyone talked at once. Their voices grew louder and louder.

"Sh-h-h!" James scolded, looking over his shoulder. "Not so loud."

Churchill nodded. "James is right. We had better keep this quiet. But you fellows keep your ears open." The men agreed. Later, when he was alone with Thomas and James, Churchill whispered, "If that story is true, there is a chance we might be in Texas by New Year's Day. Believe me, we can't leave Louisiana and this Mississippi River too soon for me."

"Me neither," Thomas mumbled, thinking of his wife and son. Before the week was over the news was out: Colonel Waller's battalion had orders to join General Green's division, which was already on the way to Texas! The battalion lost no time getting things together to leave Louisiana. They managed to overtake Green's division before it reached Houston on Christmas morning.

"Men," Colonel Waller said after they made camp at Houston. "I know it has been almost two years since most of you have seen your loved ones. Many of you live not far from here. If you had a five-day furlough you could get home and back and still have a few days with your families, couldn't you?"

The men cheered loudly at the thought of going home.

"We will let a few men at a time go from each company. When one group returns the next can leave." Colonel Waller added, "I have no way of knowing how long we will be here at Houston or where we will be sent from here. Make good use of your time."

Everyone listened eagerly as the names were read. The names of Churchill and Thomas were on the first list. Churchill was disappointed that his brother had to wait, but there was nothing he could do.

On the way home Churchill wrestled with the question: Should he see his mother first or should he visit Susan? Thomas encouraged him to visit his family first. He suggested Churchill meet him at David Randon's later. They could ride to Susan's home together that afternoon. Churchill agreed with the plan.

When they reached the fork in the road, Thomas waved goodbye and galloped homeward to his wife and son. Churchill glanced longingly toward Susan's when he came to Mill Creek, but he went on.

Nearing home, a lump rose in Churchill's throat. He watched the smoke from the chimney curling lazily into the crisp morning air. Home! He was home at last!

As Churchill rode into the yard a small hound dog ran around from the back of the house. The dog barked wildly while Churchill tied his horse to the hitching post. The dog howled louder when Churchill tried to pet it. There was something about the animal that reminded him of Thumper when he was young. The door of the cabin burst open before Churchill stepped upon the porch.

"Oh, son, it is you! You're home!" his mother exclaimed, throwing her arms around his neck. She cried with happiness as Churchill caught her in his arms and lifted her off the ground in a big hug. As he put her down, Churchill grabbed Harriet, Amanda, and Sarah to swing them around.

"Mercy it's cold out here. Let's go inside," Elizabeth insisted. Marcus and Billy ran from the barn to see what all the noise was about. Churchill could not believe that

Billy had grown so tall. Churchill had always thought of him as a little boy, but Billy was now a man.

The girls pushed and shoved, trying to crawl into Churchill's lap as the family gathered around the table. Everyone wanted to talk at once. Finally, Marcus laughingly raised his hand for silence. "Whoa! Just a minute. Let's take turns — one question at a time. That'll give Churchill a chance to answer. All right, Betsy, you start."

"Where's your brother? Is he all right?"

Churchill assured his mother that James was fine and that he would be coming home in a few days.

While he told them of his adventures, Churchill was secretly enjoying the warm, cozy kitchen and the cheery fire in the fireplace. The tantalizing fragrance from the pot of stew simmering on the hot coals reminded Churchill he was hungry. He had not eaten since he and Thomas left Houston. They had been too eager to get home to stop for food. Churchill never knew anything could taste so good as his mother's fresh buttered cornbread and the bowl of steaming stew.

Billy insisted that Churchill ride his horse when he put on his coat to go to Susan's. Churchill was grateful. His own horse was tired after the long journey. The puppy began barking as Churchill walked outside.

"Where did he come from?" Churchill asked.

"Mr. Randon gave him to Mama and the girls," Billy smiled. "And he is one of Thumper's puppies."

Churchill chuckled softly as he rode away, "Well, I'll be." Thomas and his wife and son were already at the Randons when Churchill arrived. He was happy to see his friends, but Churchill was eager to see Susan.

"Son, I know you want to see my niece," David Randon said, patting Churchill's arm understandingly. "But, if you don't mind, I thought Nancy and I would go along. Lewis is hitching up the buggy and Hattie's packing a basket of food to take. When we get to my sister's we can all hear your stories — it'll save you boys having to tell

your stories twice." The old man's eyes twinkled knowingly as he added, "By the way, Churchill, you will want
to see your dogs. I reckon they can come along. Besides,
Thumper and Tiny need the exercise. Perhaps you and
Susan will find time to take them hunting while you are
home. Lewis will bring your dogs around when he brings
the buggy."

It was not long before they heard Thumper and Tiny
scratching and yelping mournfully at the door. They
were wild with excitement. The hounds had caught
Churchill's scent. When Thomas opened the door, Thumper shot forward, knocking Churchill off of his feet.
Churchill found himself on the floor with the dogs lick-
ing his face. Thomas's young son, Algier, squealed with
glee. Everyone laughed.

After the excitement had settled, the group moved
out to the buggy. With it so crowded, Churchill insisted
on riding ahead with the dogs. He would wait for the
buggy at the bend in the road.

The dogs frolicked happily back and forth in front of
the horse. With the cold wind in his face and the sweet
smell of the woods around him, war somehow seemed far
away. Churchill slid to the ground. With his arms around
Thumper and Tiny, he muttered softly, "It is great to be
home."

"Come on," Thomas shouted, rousing Churchill from
his thoughts.

Churchill had dreamed of surprising Susan, but her
mother heard them coming. Elizabeth Newman ran into
the yard to welcome them with open arms.

"Where's Susan?" Churchill asked impatiently when
he had a chance.

"She's in the barn seeing about her horse. We can
call her."

"Never mind, Mrs. Newman. I'll go out there,"
Churchill said, tying his horse to the post. "Maybe I can
surprise her after all. Now you dogs be quiet. Don't you

make a sound, you hear?" Thumper cocked his head to one side and raised his ears knowingly.

Churchill tiptoed around the corner of the house with the hounds right behind him. "Sh-h-h," he whispered, slowly opening the barn door to peer inside. Susan did not see him because she had her arms full of hay, with her back to the door.

"The yellow rose of Texas . . ." The words of the song froze in Susan's throat. She had a strange feeling that she was not alone. "Mother, is that . . ." She did not finish. Her mouth flew open in surprise as she turned around. The hay flew in all directions. She ran toward Churchill, crying, "Is it you? Is it really you?" She flung herself into Churchill's arms.

Sometime later they joined the others, who were crowded around the kitchen table. With all the excitement, no one noticed the dogs curled quietly by Churchill's feet or Susan's hand resting in his.

"It's like a party," little Algier squealed, watching the women unpack the delicious-looking food from the basket. Everyone agreed.

Churchill was content to let Thomas do most of the talking. He told of his battalion losing their horses and equipment in the swamps of Louisiana. He told of the battles they had fought and of his buddies who had been wounded or captured by the Yankees. He carefully avoided mentioning the number that had been killed. Since they would be returning to battle, Thomas saw no need to alarm his family. Thomas concluded by saying, "The colonel let us come home for a few days. Once we get back to camp, another group will leave. Churchill's brother will be coming in a few days."

"And after that?" his uncle asked.

Thomas shrugged his shoulders. "Who knows? Let's not think of that, Uncle David. We'll enjoy the time we have together."

Churchill nodded. He noticed how David Randon had aged. His black hair was now silvery gray. His eyes had lost their twinkle, and his hands were no longer steady. "Mr. Randon," Churchill said slowly, "How are things with you?"

Sighing deeply, the man tried in vain to be unconcerned as he said, "Well frankly, boy, they're not so good. Some of my workers have run away, and I worry about the others. If the North should win this war, what will happen to them? I've been like a father to most of them. They cannot read or write. The only thing they know is working the land. I would free them today if I could be sure they would be all right. I don't worry about Nancy or myself. We would get along somehow, even though it wouldn't be easy. You know, I sold most of my horses to the army. I kept only a few. I don't know how we would manage planting and harvesting. But I reckon the good Lord would take care of that." David Randon glanced out the window. "Goodness, the day is almost over. We had better be heading home. Will you come with us, boy?"

"I'm sorry, sir, but my family is expecting me," Churchill said. While the others gathered their things, Churchill looked at Susan. "I'll be back around noon tomorrow. Maybe we can go for a ride down by the creek." He kissed her lightly on the cheek.

After telling his mother and sister goodbye, Thomas helped the others into the buggy. "Churchill, I'll meet you at Uncle David's day after tomorrow."

Churchill nodded. "And I will bring back my dogs, Mr. Randon. It's mighty nice of you to keep them for me." He knew they must leave by noon of the third day in order to be back at Houston before their furloughs expired. "See you tomorrow, Susan. Goodbye everybody." Churchill and the dogs faded into the darkness.

Churchill fell asleep that night thinking of Susan. He had no way of knowing when the war would end or what might happen to him. He longed to take Susan for his wife, but he knew that would have to wait until the war was over.

The next morning was cold and damp. Churchill

helped milk the cows and feed the horses. Marcus decided it was a fine morning to sit around the fire and visit. While the men talked about the war, the girls churned the butter and helped their mother. Betsy looked up from her work occasionally to ask a question. Flames from the fire cast a warm red glow into the corners. The cozy kitchen was filled with the delicious aroma of soup boiling on the hot coals.

Churchill sighed contentedly. Memories of sleeping on the wet, marshy ground in Louisiana with an empty stomach seemed a lifetime away. "If I could only bottle some of this and take it with me," he said wistfully. "I sure have missed your laughter and teasing. I'll be glad when this war is over."

"So will I, son," his mother said. "Billy, would you get me some water while the girls are setting the table?"

Churchill volunteered to help. He took the buckets from the shelf and handed one of them to his brother. On the way back from the well, Billy said, "I sure would like to go with you."

Churchill frowned. "No! James and I will do the fighting. You stay in the home guards with Marcus to protect Ma and the girls. The Yankees might come this way before it's all over."

Later, on the way to Susan's, Churchill wondered what he might say to discourage Billy from thinking of going with him.

Susan ran from the house and leaped on her horse when she saw Churchill coming around the bend. "I was afraid you weren't coming," she cried, riding up to meet him. "Come on. I'll race you."

Churchill grabbed the reins before Susan could move. "No you don't, young lady," he laughed. "We'll go together." They rode side by side down to the creek. Tiny darted in and out among the weeds while they sat and talked. Suddenly, they heard a spine-tingling howl.

"Listen, that's Thumper. Tiny hears him too. Come on. Let's see what he has treed. It's a good thing Billy left me this," Churchill said as he unstrapped the gun from the saddle. They zigzagged in and out among the trees, with Tiny in the lead. As they neared the creek bank, Tiny froze with his tail pointed in the air. Churchill saw Thumper at the base of a nearby tree. A big raccoon was clinging to one of the branches. Churchill raised his gun and fired. The hounds barked wildly when the raccoon tumbled to the ground. Churchill made sure the creature was dead before he picked it up. "I'll bet your mother will make some fine stew with this. Well, I reckon we had better head back. Besides," Churchill scanned the skies, "it's going to rain."

A fine mist was falling by the time they reached the house. They spread their coats on the hearth to dry and huddled near the fire to get warm.

Night was falling when Churchill kissed Susan goodbye and started home.

The next morning he bade his family farewell and rode off toward Mr. Randon's house. Thumper and Tiny howled and whined when they were put in their cages. They had enjoyed their freedom. Churchill could hear Thumper's pitiful cry as he and Thomas rode off toward Houston. He was grateful that Billy had decided to remain home a little longer.

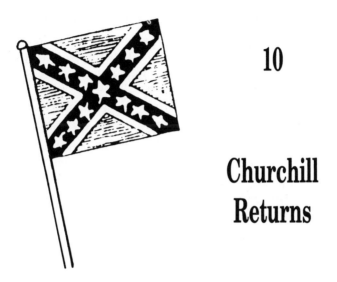

10

Churchill Returns

In his thoughts Churchill relived each moment of his visit with Susan. His heart ached, knowing he was such a short distance from her and yet could not be with her. His battalion had been told that they would move on a moment's notice.

One evening Churchill looked at Thomas thoughtfully. "I hate this waiting. Do you think we will be moving soon?"

"Yes, I do!" Thomas replied. "It's rumored that the Union forces under General Nathaniel Banks are marching northward from New Orleans. At the same time, a fleet of Yankee ships is supposed to sail up the Red River. The two units will meet and head this way. If that is true, and the Yankees do plan on invading Texas, I reckon we will get orders to stop them. I only hope we can."

Thomas was right. Waller's battalion received orders to proceed to Alexandria, Louisiana. Before they could reach the city, they learned that Alexandria had fallen to the enemy. Waller's scouts reported that a number of Union soldiers were camped a short distance away. The colonel decided to wait for General Richard Taylor and his men. On April 8, 1864, the Confederate and Union armies met at a place they called Sabine-Crossroads. The Southerners claimed victory, but both sides lost many men. The two armies met again at Pleasant Hill. In spite of their victory that day, the Union leaders decided to abandon their plan to invade Texas.

From May to September, Churchill's battalion fought in a number of minor battles. Names of the places ran together in Churchill's head. In Louisiana there were battles at Mansura, Moroville, Yellow Bayou, McNutt's Hill, and many other places.

When they were not fighting, the men were patrolling the area. One morning they chanced upon what had once been a beautiful plantation home nestled among a grove of tall trees. "Look at that house! I never saw one that big before!" Churchill exclaimed. "It's like a palace. Wouldn't Ma love that, James?"

"She sure would. Imagine living in a two-story house! Who do you suppose lived there?"

Thomas spoke up. "I heard it belongs to some fellow who raised sugar cane before the war. The house is supposed to have sixteen rooms! And look at the gardens. My Mary would love those flowers. Just look at the azaleas and camelias! The place looks deserted, but the flowers are blooming." The garden was a riot of color in spite of the weeds.

"And look at those trees!" Churchill said, pointing to the stately oaks draped with moss. He could see the remains of the burned sugar houses behind the bigger home. The fences had been flattened and the barns ransacked. The charred beds and wheels were all that remained of the wagons.

Churchill shook his head sadly. What had once been a place of beauty had been brought to desolation. With the plantation owner away, fighting in the army, there was little the women and children could do to stop the enemy from taking their horses and cows and whatever else they wanted. Churchill muttered, "How sad that people worked and struggled all their lives and now this!"

Churchill had no way of knowing that scores of other plantations across the South, as well as farms in the North, had also been destroyed by the ravages of war.

Waller's battalion moved north from Louisiana up to Arkansas in mid-September. They had not been there long when they met the Union soldiers. After that battle on September 27, 1864, at DeVall's Bluff on the White River, they set up camp at Fulton.

One day a wounded soldier limped into camp. They crowded around to hear the latest news. The man said, "Did you hear that Abraham Lincoln has been re-elected president of the United States?"

"I'm not surprised," someone replied. "What else is new?"

"Well," the soldier continued, "on November 15, General William Sherman and his Union army burned Atlanta, Georgia. I understand that Sherman is bragging he'll burn everything in his path as he marches to the sea. I hope he is wrong."

A few days later the weather turned cold. Churchill and his buddies huddled around the campfire, trying to keep warm. His battered hat was pulled down over his ears to protect them from the cold. Churchill tried to keep his teeth from chattering. He rubbed his hands together to keep them warm. "Oh, for those hot summer days in Texas! If I ever get warm, I will never complain about being too hot again. Never!"

"Me neither," his brother groaned. "The cold rain is bad enough, but it's the sleet I hate. It was so cold last night there were icicles on my nose when I woke up. The bottoms of my shoes are so thin my feet are numb."

"Mine too." Thomas laughed grimly. "Well, at least we aren't alone. The Yankees are freezing too. I just hope we move out of this place before we all freeze to death. Lord," his eyes moved heavenward, "deliver me from Arkansas!"

Thomas's prayer was answered. Waller's battalion, along with General Green's men, were ordered back to Texas. Once they crossed the Sabine River, Churchill vowed he felt warmer.

They made camp not far from the little town of Alto on the Neches River. While they were there, they learned that General Robert E. Lee had been made commander-in-chief of the Confederate armies.

As soon as Churchill and his comrades were settled, they were ordered to move again. Before many days had passed they had moved from Alto Springs to Hall's Bluff to Crockett and, finally, to Hempstead. Once they reached Hempstead, Churchill shook his head. "I cannot believe this is where we started out in the army. Was it only three years ago? It seems like a lifetime."

Thomas sighed wearily. "If the colonel would let us, we could be home in no time."

"Well, he ain't gonna let you go, so don't go thinking of leaving — not yet!" one of the men replied.

News came thick and fast: General Robert E. Lee had surrendered the Confederate army of Northern Virginia on April 9, 1865. A few days later, on April 14, President Abraham Lincoln was shot. He died the next day. The last battle of the war took place near Brownsville, Texas, on May 13. But the best news of all came on May 20. Colonel Edwin Waller's battalion and the other Confederate divisions in Texas were disbanded. The men were free to go home! The South had suffered a great defeat, but the Civil War was over!

Churchill and his friends grabbed their gear and headed home. On the way, Churchill looked from his brother to Thomas and laughed. "You know, they might mistake us for Yankees if we don't wash up and comb our hair. We look pretty wild."

"I reckon we do at that," Thomas chuckled. They

paused at the creek long enough to water their horses and wash their faces. Then they rode on to the bend in the road.

"James, tell Ma I will see her later. I'm going to Susan's now!"

Thomas yelled back over his shoulder, "And I am going home!" As Churchill came around the bend, he saw Susan chopping wood near the side of her house. She looked up and saw him riding toward her. With a loud cry, Susan dropped the ax and ran toward him with outstretched arms. Through her happiness and tears she cried, "Oh, Churchill, you're home! You have come back to me!"

Churchill leaped from his horse and took her in his arms. "Yes," he promised, as he kissed and hugged her, "and this Texas Rebel will never leave you again!"

Glossary

BLOCKADE: the closing of a port to prevent ships or troops from entering or leaving.

BULL RUN: small river near Manassas, Virginia. Site of two battles (1861 and 1862) where Union forces were defeated.

BUMPER CROP: an abundant crop.

CHICKAMAUGA *(chik'a-mo'ga)* Cherokee word meaning "River of Death." Located in Georgia near Tennessee border. Site of battle (1863).

CONFEDERATE STATES OF AMERICA: the eleven Southern states which seceded from the Union in 1860–1861.

FEDERALIST: Northern states which did not secede from the Union.

FORT BEND COUNTY (Texas): located on Brazos River where Stephen F. Austin's first colony settled in 1823. Richmond is the county seat.

FORT SUMTER: near Charleston, South Carolina. Site of first Civil War battle (April 12, 1861) where Confederates defeated Unionists.

GRANT, ULYSSES S. (1822–1885): Union general and eighteenth president of the U.S. (1869–1877).

LEE, ROBERT E. (1807–1870): Confederate general. Surrendered to Grant at Appomattox, Virginia (April 9, 1865).

MISSISSIPPI RIVER: principal river of the U.S. which flows from Minnesota to the Gulf of Mexico.

NORTH: states lying north of the Ohio River, Missouri, and Maryland, which fought with the Union in Civil War.

REBEL: name given to the Confederate soldiers of the South.

SECEDE: to separate from a political union or federation.

SHILOH: site of bloody battle (April 1862) where General

Grant forced the Confederates to retreat to Corinth, Mississippi.

TERRY, BENJAMIN FRANK: hero leader of Terry's Texas Rangers from Fort Bend County. Was killed at Woodsonville, Kentucky (December 17, 1861).

UNION: Northern states which did not secede in the Civil War.

YANKEE: name given to Federal or Unionist soldiers.